CD INCLUDED

CD INSIDE
FRONT COVER

PIANO · VOCAL

BROADWAY SINGER'S edition

VOCAL WITH PIANO ACCOMPANIMENT

Boublil and Schönberg's

Les Misérables™

ISBN 978-1-4768-1422-3

ALAIN BOUBLIL MUSIC LTD.

EXCLUSIVELY DISTRIBUTED BY

HAL·LEONARD®
CORPORATION

7777 W. BLUEMOUND RD. P.O. BOX 13819 MILWAUKEE, WI 53213

Pianists on the CD: [1] Brian Dean [2] Jamie Johns [3] Richard Walters

At the End of the Day

Music by CLAUDE-MICHEL SCHÖNBERG
Lyrics by ALAIN BOUBLIL, JEAN-MARC NATEL
and HERBERT KRETZMER

THE POOR:

At the end of the day you're an-oth-er day old-er,

and that's all you can say for the life of the poor. It's a

strug-gle, __ it's a war, and there's noth-ing that an-y-one's giv-ing. One more

GIRL 1: Have you seen how the fore-man is fum-ing to - day,

with his ter - ri - ble breath and his wan-der-ing hands?

GIRL 2: It's be-cause lit - tle Fan-tine won't give him his way. GIRL 1: Take a look at his trou-sers, you see where he

stands. GIRL 4: And the boss, he ___ nev - er knows that the

Bb
cir - cus. Now, come on, la - dies, set - tle down.
F(add2)

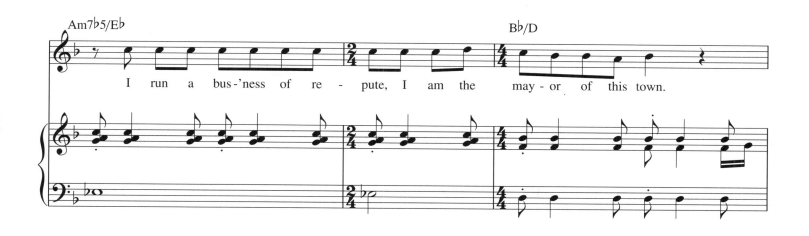

Am7b5/Eb
I run a bus-'ness of re - pute, I am the may - or of this town.
Bb/D

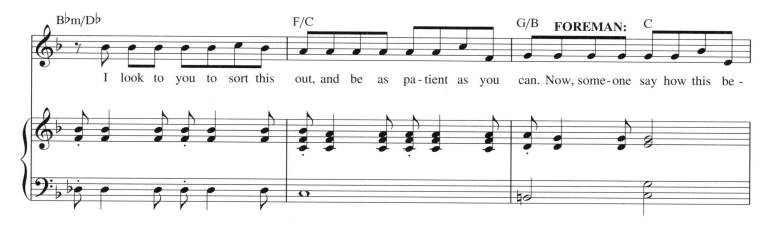

Bbm/Db
I look to you to sort this out, and be as pa - tient as you can. Now, some-one say how this be -
F/C   G/B   **FOREMAN:** C

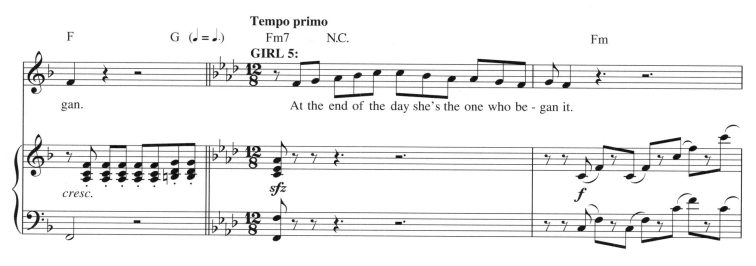

Tempo primo
F   G (♩ = ♩.)   Fm7   N.C.   Fm
GIRL 5:
gan. At the end of the day she's the one who be - gan it.
cresc.   *sfz*   *f*

20

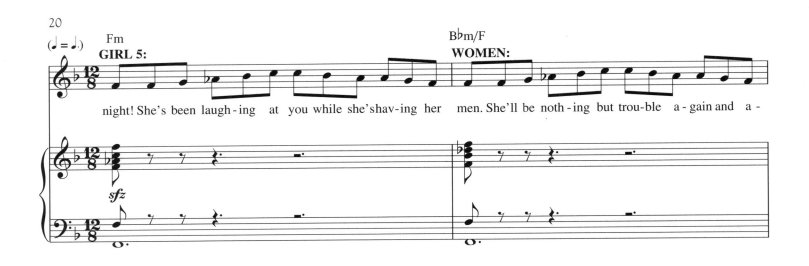

Bring Him Home

Music by CLAUDE-MICHEL SCHÖNBERG
Lyrics by HERBERT KRETZMER and ALAIN BOUBLIL

Castle on a Cloud

Music by CLAUDE-MICHEL SCHÖNBERG
Lyrics by ALAIN BOUBLIL, JEAN-MARC NATEL
and HERBERT KRETZMER

Do You Hear the People Sing?

Music by CLAUDE-MICHEL SCHÖNBERG
Lyrics by ALAIN BOUBLIL, JEAN-MARC NATEL
and HERBERT KRETZMER

31

life a- bout to start when to- mor- row comes. Will you

FEUILLY:

give all you can give so that our ban - ner may ad- vance? Some will

fall and some will live. Will you stand up and take your chance? The

blood of the mar- tyrs will wa - ter the mead- ows of France! Do you

ALL:

Drink with Me
(To Days Gone By)

Music by CLAUDE-MICHEL SCHÖNBERG
Lyrics by HERBERT KRETZMER and ALAIN BOUBLIL

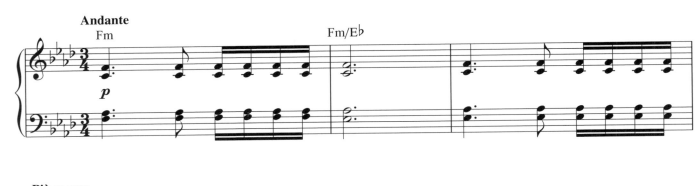

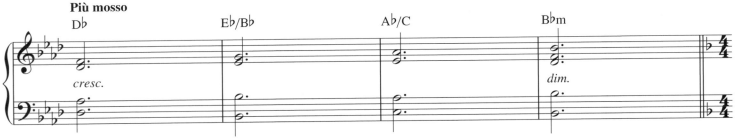

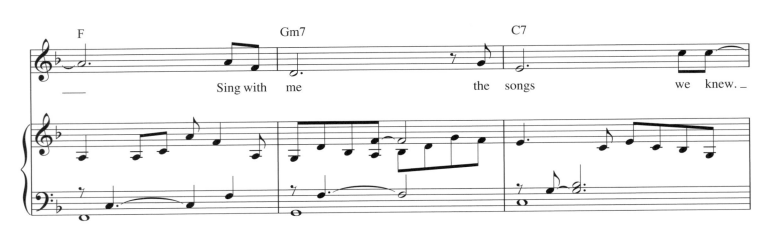

35

A Little Fall of Rain

Music by CLAUDE-MICHEL SCHÖNBERG
Lyrics by ALAIN BOUBLIL, JEAN-MARC NATEL
and HERBERT KRETZMER

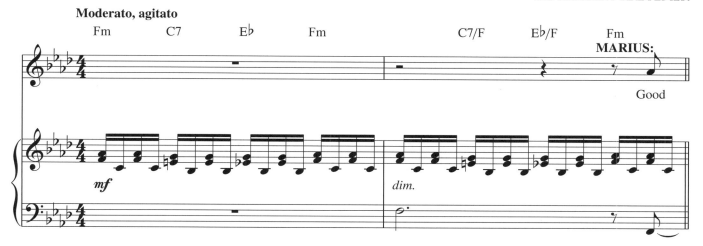

where you are, ____ I've come home from so far.

Più lento (in 8)

So don't you fret, M'sieur Mar - ius, __ I don't feel an - y pain. A

MARIUS:

Hush - a - bye, ____ dear É - po - nine, you won't feel an - y pain. A

lit - tle fall of rain can hard - ly hurt me now. That's all I need to

lit - tle fall of rain can hard - ly hurt you now. I'm here.

know. And you will keep me safe and you will keep me close, and

I will stay with you _ till you are sleep - ing.

rain will make the flow - ers...

And rain will make the flow-ers grow.

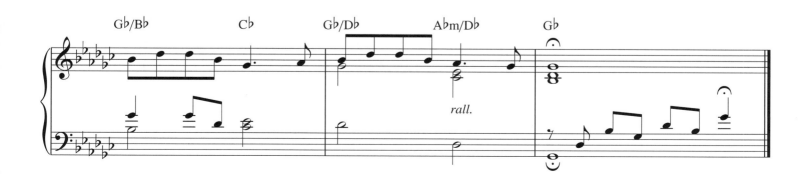

Empty Chairs at Empty Tables

Music by CLAUDE-MICHEL SCHÖNBERG
Lyrics by HERBERT KRETZMER and ALAIN BOUBLIL

A Heart Full of Love

Music by CLAUDE-MICHEL SCHÖNBERG
Lyrics by ALAIN BOUBLIL, JEAN-MARC NATEL
and HERBERT KRETZMER

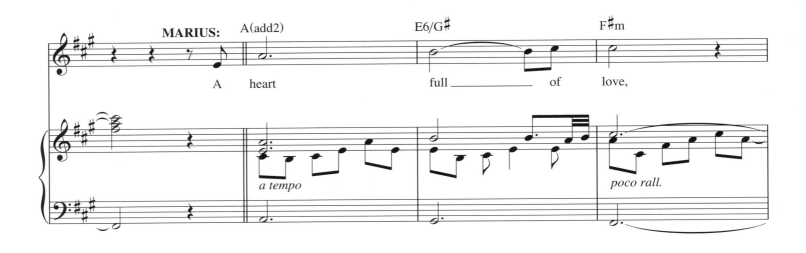

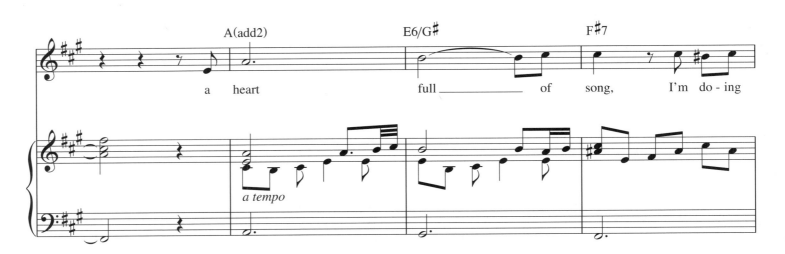

51

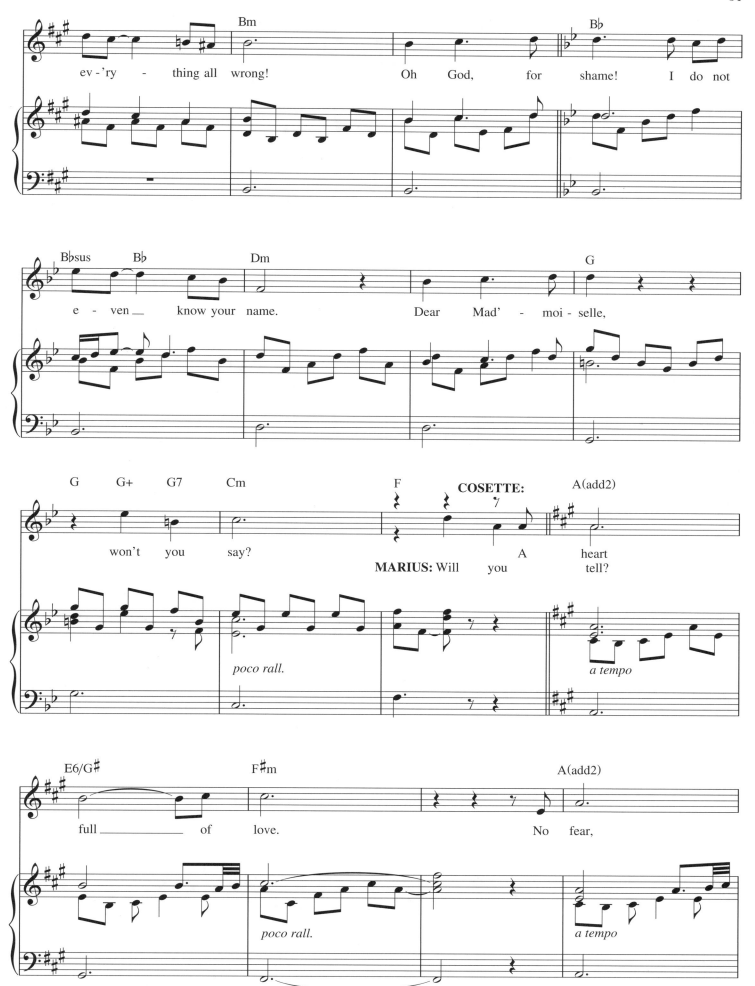

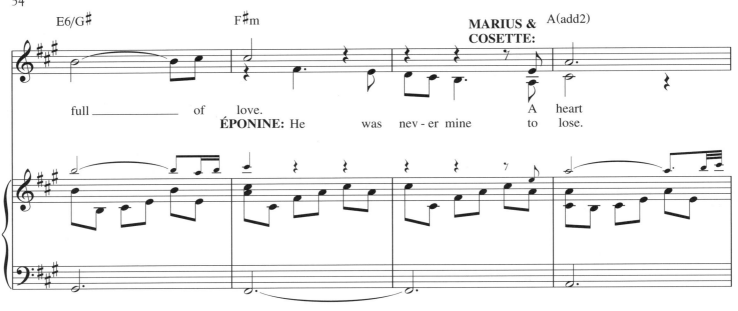

full _____ of love.

ÉPONINE: He was nev - er mine to lose.

A heart

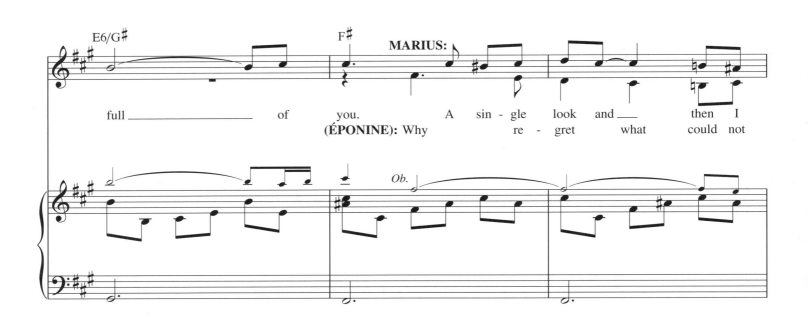

full _____ of you.

(ÉPONINE): Why re - gret what could not

A sin - gle look and ___ then I

MARIUS:

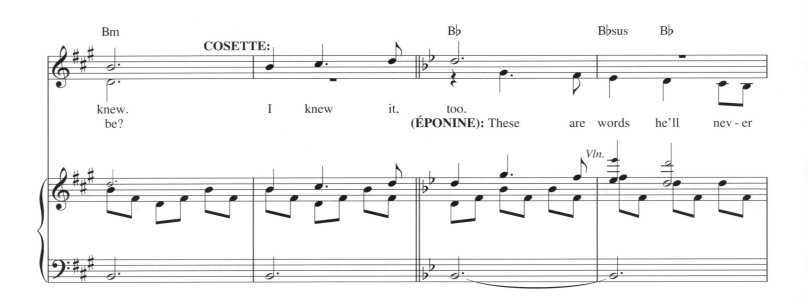

knew.

be?

COSETTE: I knew it, too.

(ÉPONINE): These are words he'll nev - er

I Dreamed a Dream

Music by CLAUDE-MICHEL SCHÖNBERG
Lyrics by ALAIN BOUBLIL, JEAN-MARC NATEL
and HERBERT KRETZMER

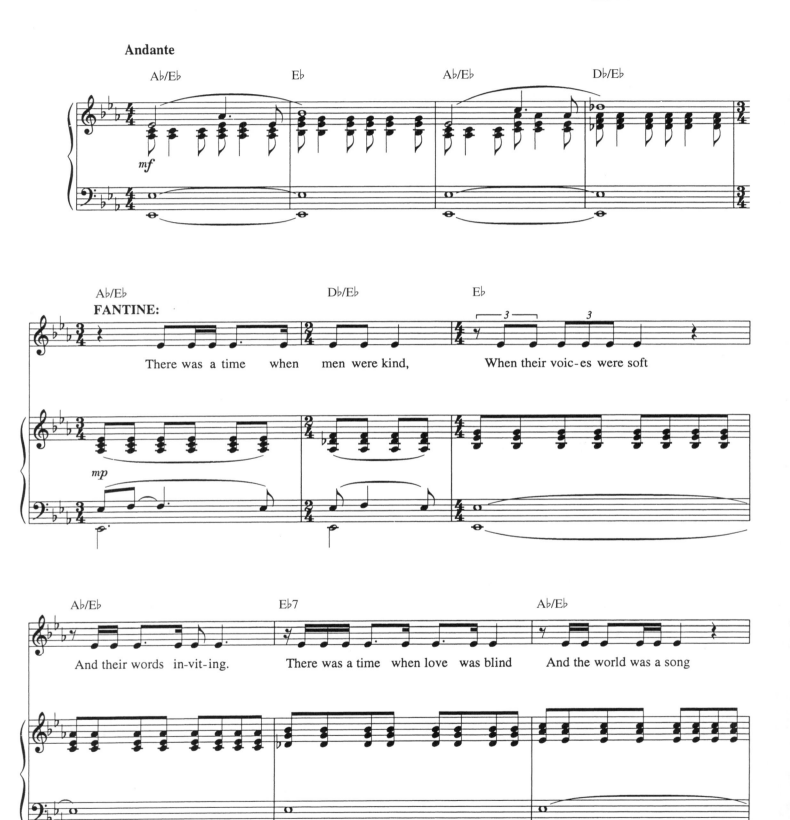

I dreamed that God would be for-giv-ing. Then I was young and un-af-

raid And dreams were made and used and wast-ed.

There was no ran-som to be paid, No song un-sung, no wine un-

Poco piú mosso

tast-ed. But the ti-gers come at night

In My Life

Music by CLAUDE-MICHEL SCHÖNBERG
Lyrics by ALAIN BOUBLIL, JEAN-MARC NATEL
and HERBERT KRETZMER

COSETTE: How strange, this feel-ing that my life's be-gun at last. This change: Can peo-ple real-ly fall in love so fast? What's the mat-ter with

Music and Lyrics Copyright © 1980 by Editions Musicales Alain Boublil
English Lyrics Copyright © 1986 by Alain Boublil Music Ltd. (ASCAP)
Mechanical and Publication Rights for the U.S.A. Administered by Alain Boublil Music Ltd. (ASCAP) c/o Joel Faden & Co., Inc.,
MLM 250 West 57th St., 26th Floor, New York, NY 10107, Tel. (212) 246-7203, Fax (212) 246-7217, mwlock@joelfaden.com
International Copyright Secured. All Rights Reserved. This music is copyright. Photocopying is illegal.
All Performance Rights Restricted.

Moderately slow

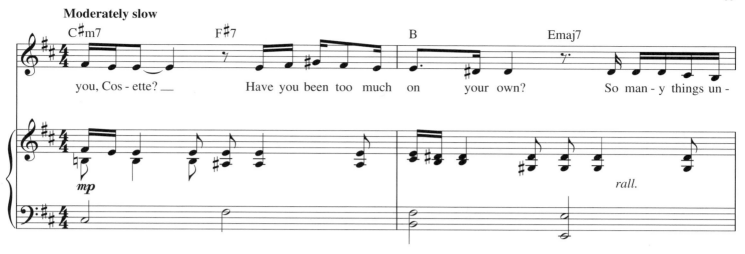

you, Cos - ette? ___ Have you been too much on your own? So man - y things un -

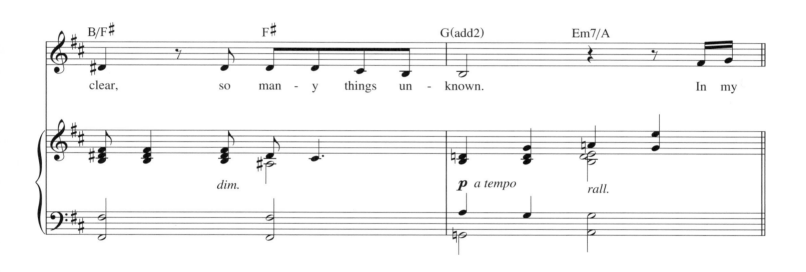

clear, so man - y things un - known. In my

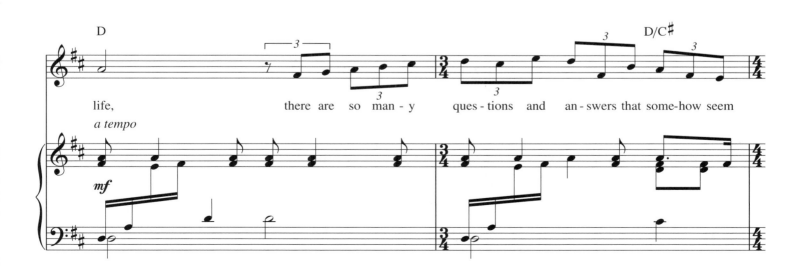

life, there are so man - y ques - tions and an - swers that some-how seem

Master of the House

Music by CLAUDE-MICHEL SCHÖNBERG
Lyrics by ALAIN BOUBLIL, JEAN-MARC NATEL
and HERBERT KRETZMER

CODA

How it all in-creas-es, all ____ them bits and piec-es, Je - sus, it's a-maz-ing how it

poco accel.

Poco più mosso
add ENSEMBLE:

grows! Mas-ter of the house, quick to catch your eye,

nev-er wants a pass-er-by to pass him by. Ser-vant to the poor,

but-ler to the great, com-fort-er, phi-los-o-pher and life-long mate.

Stars

Music by CLAUDE-MICHEL SCHONBERG
Lyrics by HERBERT KRETZMER and ALAIN BOUBLIL

81

On My Own

Music by CLAUDE-MICHEL SCHONBERG
Lyrics by ALAIN BOUBLIL, JEAN-MARC NATEL,
HERBERT KRETZMER, JOHN CAIRD and TREVOR NUNN

EPONINE: And now I'm all a-lone a-gain, no-where to turn, no one to go to.

84

Who Am I?

Music by CLAUDE-MICHEL SCHÖNBERG
Lyrics by ALAIN BOUBLIL, JEAN-MARC NATEL
and HERBERT KRETZMER

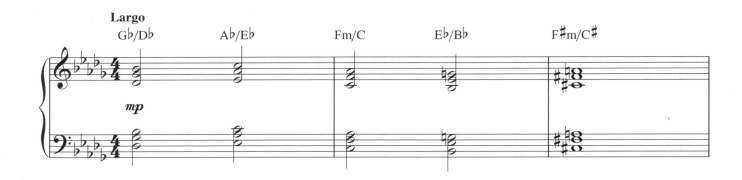

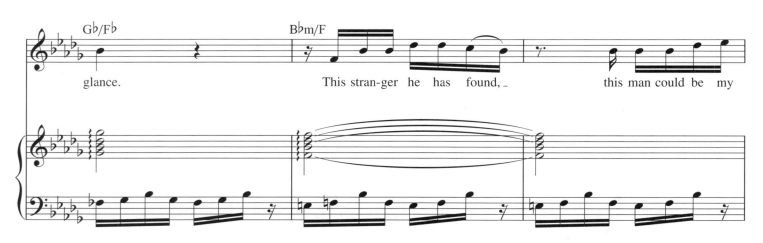